© **1994**
4th Printing 2000

ISBN: 0-89538-064-1

L-W Book Sales
PO Box 69
Gas City, Indiana 46933

INTRODUCTION

Over 100,000 magazines were published before 1900. With that in mind, you will understand how difficult it would be to have a complete book on magazine collecting. This book is an attempt to give a general overview of the field of collecting and pricing old magazines.

Some of the main reasons magazines are collected are artists' illustrations, advertisements, authors, movie stars and historical events. A person specializing in a certain field will pay a premium price for a magazine pertaining to that field. This should always be kept in mind while buying and selling.

Prices have been obtained from auction results, show results, and the opinions of many experts in the field. No doubt there will be some disagreement on prices and possibly a few mistakes. However, we do feel this price guide will give you a good guideline for purchasing and selling magazines.

AFSCA World Report
1959- $2-4

Aboriginal Science Fiction, No. 2-28 . . . . $4-5

Ace High, June 1938 . . . . $6

Ace Sports, 1930's $10

Adventure
1900-1919 . . . . $27-44
1920's $16-27
1930's $8-16
1940's $3-7

Aero Digest
1930's $10
1944-1952 . . . . $5
            Sept. 1942 . . . . $27
After Dark
1970's $6-13

Agricultural Epitomist, The, 1882- $3-5

Airbrush Action, 1988, Varga $2-5

Airlift (formerly American Aviation)
1937- $1-3

Air News, 1944-1946 . . . . $30-53

Air Progress, June & July 1943 . . . . $30-53

Air Travel News, Dec. 1928 . . . . $13

Air Wonder Stories, 1929-1930 . . . . $11-22

Alaskan Sportsman
1934-1949 . . . . $6-11
1950- $3-5

Alfred Hitchcock
     May 1960 .... $11
     January 1972 .... $5

All Pets Magazine
1934-1939 .... $3-5
1940- $1-3

Amazing Science Fiction
1920's $16-27
1930's $11-16
1940's $6-11
1950's $3-5
1960's- $1-2
     March 1941 .... $22
     June 1941 .... $22
     January 1942 .... $22
     February 1943 .... $27

Amazing Stories
August 1928 .... $38
March 1929 .... $38
May 1930 .... $38
June 1942 .... $17
May 1959 .... $7

Amazing Stories Quarterly, to 1934 .... $9-17

Americana Mag., *Nov/Dec 1978, Mickey is 50* $27

American
1898-1919 .... $22-33
1920's-1930's $22-27
1940-1956 .... $11-22

American Agriculturist
1841-1899 .... $11-16
1900-1939 .... $6-11
1940- $1-5

American Antiquity, 1935- $2-4

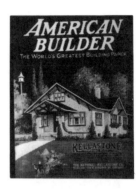

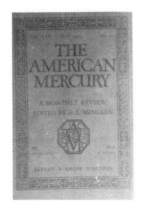

American Artist 1937- $3-7

American Bee Journal
1861-1899 . . . . $6-11
1900- $2-5

American Boy
1899-1941 . . . . $5-11

American Builder, September 1923 . . . . $2-5

American Cinematographer, 1980's $2-6

American City Magazine, The, 1967-1968 . . . . $5

American Collector, 1931- $2-5

American Farm Youth 1935- $2-5

American Field
1874-1899 . . . . $8-14
1900-1939 . . . . $6-8
1940-1949 . . . . $4-6
1950- $1-4

American Forestry
1895-1939 . . . . $2-5
1940- $1-3

American Furrier
1900-1919 . . . . $11-17
1920- $4-10

American Girl
1917-1939 . . . . $2-5
1940- $1-3
        Nov. 1955, B. Ruth $5

American Glass Review
1882-1889 . . . . $13-20
1900-1939 . . . . $8-13
1940-1949 . . . . $5-7

1950- $3-5
American Golfer, Dec. 1932 .... $10

American Heritage
1954- $2-5
      April 1968, Mickey Mouse Cover $27

American Home Magazine
1928-1939 .... $6-10
1940- 1960 .... $3-8

American Junior Red Cross News, 1950's $2-4

American Legion Magazine, October 1926. .... $25

American Legion Weekly, April 16, 1926 .... $7

American Machinist, 1878- $3-10

American Magazine
      Nov. 1918, Norman Rockwell $22-44
      March 1923, Norman Rockwell $16-33

American Mercury
1924-1929 .... $6-11
1930-1949 .... $3-5
1950- $1-3

American Mineralogist, 1916- $1-4

American Needlewoman, 1923 .... $7

American Neptune
1941-1949 .... $5-10
1950- $3-5

American Philatelist, 1886- $2-5

American Poultry Journal
1874-1929 .... $6-11

American Poultry Journal (Continued)
1930-1949 . . . . $2-5
1950- $1-3

American Printer, The, Feb. 1933 . . . . $8

American Review of Reviews, Nov. 1921 . . . . $10

American Rifleman
1885-1899 . . . . $11-16
1900-1939 . . . . $6-11
1940's. $4
1950-1960 . . . . $3
1970-. $2

American Rodding, 1960's $3-5

American Sportsman
1968-1970. . . . . $6-11
    Vol. 3 #1, Winter. $33
    Vol. 3 #2, Spring. $33

American Sunday Monthly, 1914-1915. . . . . $33
    Dec. 1914. . . . . $44

American Teacher, 1880's $6-11

American Woman, The
1920's $6-11
    April 1922, Little Women Paper Dolls $27
    Nov. 1922 . . . . $22

America's Humor, Sept. 1928 . . . . $9

Antique Automobile, 1960's $5-9

Antiquarian, The, 1916- $3-8

Antiques
1920's-1939 . . . . $9-13
1940-1959 . . . . $3-6
1960- $1-3

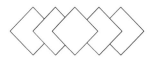

Apollo
1925-1949 . . . . $8-12
1950- $2-7

Appalachia
1907-1939 . . . . $3-6
1940- $1-3

Appleton's Book Lover's Magazine, 1907- $3-5

Aquatic Life, 1910's $4-10

Arabian Horse News, 1948- $1-4

Archaeology, 1948- $2-5

Arctic, 1948- $2-5

Argonaut, The, 1870- $5-15

Argosy
1882-1909 . . . . $22-33
1910-1939 . . . . $11-22
1940-1949 . . . . $6-11
1950- $2-5

Arizona and the West, 1959- $1-4

Arizona Farmer – Ranchman
1922-1939 . . . . $3-8
1940- $1-3

Arizona Highways
1925-1949 . . . . $6-11
1950- $3-5

Arthur's New Home Magazine, 1850-1898 . . . . $6-11

Art News
1902-1939 . . . . $4-8
1940- $1-4

Art Photography, *Oct. 1954, Marilyn Monroe* $93

Art Quarterly, 1938- $3-8

Arts and Architecture
1911-1939 . . . . $3-6
1940- $1-4

Arts and Decoration, *Nov. 1922, Xavier* $32

Arts, Fads, Modes, 1920's $22

Arts and Vanities, 1920's $22

Asia, 1900- $5-11

Assay, 1945- (1 or 2 issues per year) $2-5

Astonishing Stories, 1940's $11-16

Astronomical Journal
1849-1899 . . . . $9-16
1900-1939 . . . . $5-11
1940- $2-5

Astounding Stories of Super Science, 1930 . . . . $32

Atlantic City Auditorium, June 1930 . . . . $10

Atlantic Monthly
1857-1899 . . . . $8-15
1900-1949 . . . . $4-8
1950- $1-3
          June 1921, Maxfield Parrish $44

Audubon Magazine
1899-1939 . . . . $4-8
1940- $2-4

Auk – American Ornithologists Union
1876-1899 . . . . $5-10
1900-1939 . . . . $3-5
1940- $1-3

Auto Age, 1950's $4-6

Auto Mechanics, 1956-1957. . . . . $3

Automobile Trade Journal
1899-1909 . . . . $27-44
1910-1929 . . . . $16-27
1930-1939 . . . . $11-16
1940-1949 . . . . $6-11
1950- $1-5

Avant Garde, March 1968, Marilyn $55

Aviation Week
June 1959 . . . . $16
     July 22, 1963 Manned Space Flight $27

Baseball Digest
1940's $6-11
     1948 – Musial Cover $22

Bay View Magazine, The, Dec. 1907 . . . . $4

Beauty & Health
June 1902 . . . . $5
January 1903 . . . . $5

Better Homes & Gardens
1922-1939 . . . . $6-11
1940-1949 . . . . $3-6
1950- $1-4
     Jan. 1940, Walt Disney, ... $33

Bicycle Journal
1948-1959 . . . . $3-6
1960- $1-3

Big Magazine, The, March (black cat),1930s $5

Big Song Magazine, *Sept. 1942, Davis/Van* $11

Billboard, The,
1888-1899 . . . . $11-22
1900-1949 . . . . $6-11
1950-1961 . . . . $3-5
1961- $2-4

Birds, 1895-1900 . . . . $11-22

Blood – Horse
1917-1939 . . . . $4-10
1940- $1-4

Blue Book
1904-1929 . . . . $11-22
1930-1951 . . . . $4-10
1953 . . . . $3

Boeing Magazine
1930-1939 . . . . $5-9
1940-1959 . . . . $3-5
1960- $1-3

Bohemian Magazine, The, July, 1908 . . . . $5

Boilermakers – Blacksmiths Journal
1888-1899 . . . . $13-24
1900-1929 . . . . $8-13
1930-1939 . . . . $4-7
1940- $2-4

Book Buyers Guide
1897-1939 . . . . $6-11
1940- $2-5
     Dec. 1897, Parrish $110
     Dec. 1899, Parrish $110

Booklovers Magazine, The, 1903-1906 . . . . $11-22

Bookman, The, 1895-1933 . . . . $6-11

Book Review Digest
1905-1939 .... $2-4
1940- $1-2

Bookseller, The, *May 1, 1914, Parrish* $32

Borzoi Quarterly, 1952- $1-3

Boston Cooking School Magazine
1896-1929 .... $6-11
1930- $2-5

Botanical Gazette
1875-1899 .... $6-11
1900-1929 .... $3-5
1930- $1-3

Bottle Trader, The
1971-1973 .... $2-4
            1st Issue $11

Box Office
1920-1929 .... $11-16
1930-1949 .... $6-11
1950- $2-4

Boy's Adventure Magazine, Oct. 1936 .... $32

Boy's Life
1912-1939 .... $9-13
1940-1949 .... $3-6
1950- $1-3
            May 1915, Norman Rockwell $65
            Aug. 1915, Norman Rockwell $65
            August 1959, Mantle Cover $11
            Feb. 1965, Rockwell Cover $16

Boy Scout Magazine, 1939 .... $27

Breeders Gazette, The
1881-1899 .... $6-12
1900-1939 .... $4-6
1940- $1-4

Brewers Digest
1926-1939 . . . . $2-5
1940- $1-3

Bricklayer, Mason and Plasterer
1898-1919 . . . . $3-5
1920- $1-3

Brides Magazine, 1934- $2-5

Broadcasting
1931-1939 . . . . $3-5
1940- $1-3

Broadcast Weekly, Feb. 1930 . . . . $16

Brown Jug, The, *Nov. 1922, Brown University* $5

Building and Loan News, 1885- $2-5

Business Screen
1938-1949 . . . . $2-4
1950- $1-2

Business Week
1929-1949 . . . . $3-5
1950- $1-3

Camera
1922-1939 . . . . $5-9
1940- $2-4

Camping Magazine
1926-1939 . . . . $2-5
1940- $1-3

Captain Future, 1940-1942 . . . . $11-27

Car Classics, 1966-1970 . . . . $4-8

Car Craft, 1953-1959 . . . . $4-8

Car Life, 1955-1960 . . . . $3

Carlife & Motorist, 1955 . . . . $3

Carpenter, The, 1930-1931 . . . . $16-22

Carpentry and Building, 1878- $9-16

Castle of Frankenstein
1962-1975 . . . . $16-22
    No. 1 . . . . $32
    No. 2, Christopher Lee $32
    No. 3, The Karloff story $32

Cats, 1945- $1-3

Cattlemen
1914-1939 . . . . $4-7
1940- $2-4

Cavalcade, May 1937 . . . . $5

Cavalier, The
1909-1913 . . . . $22-42
1950's-1960 . . . . $6-16
1960's-1970's $3
    May 1959, Errol Flynn $27

Central Railway Chronicle
1893-1919 . . . . $6-11
1920-1939 . . . . $3-5
1940- $1-3

Century, The
1881-1899 . . . . $16-22
1900-1930 . . . . $11-16
    Dec. 1914, Parrish $50

Chicago Field, 1871- $4-10

Child Life
1921-1939 . . . . $5-10

Child Life (Continued)
1940-49 . . . . $3-5
1950- $1-3
     Dec. 1954, Norman Rockwell $22

China, Glass and Table Wares
1892-1899 . . . . $11-16
1900-1929 . . . . $7-13
1930-1949 . . . . $5-9
1950- $1-4

Christian Herald
1878-1899 . . . . $9-16
1900-1939 . . . . $5-9
1940- $1-4

Churchman Magazines, 1904-1905 . . . . $3-5
     1904 Easter $11

Cinema Arts
     Vol. 1 #1, June 1937 . . . . $55
     Vol. 1 #2, July 1937 . . . . $32
     Vol. 1 #3, Sept. 1937 . . . . $27

Circus Review, 1953- $2-5

Classic, Aug. 1924 . . . . $22

Classmate, 1900- $2-5

Click, The National Picture Monthly Magazine
1937-1939 . . . . $11-16
1940-1944 . . . . $7-11

Clyde Beatty Circus Magazine, 1940's $11-16

Coins, 1965-1976 . . . . $3

College Humor, Sept. 1928 . . . . $11

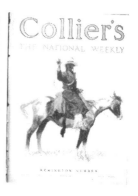

Collier's

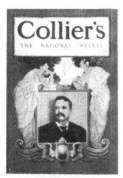

**Collier's
March 4, 1905**

Collier's
May 6, 1905

Collier's
July 1, 1905

**Collier's
July 22, 1905**

**Collier's
September 23, 1905**

**Collier's
October 14, 1905**

Collier's
October 28, 1905

**Collier's
November 18, 1905**

Collier's
January 6, 1906

Collier's
February 10, 1906

Collier's
March 10, 1906

Collier's
May 19, 1906

Collier's
June 23, 1906

Collier's
July 7, 1906

Collier's
July 21, 1906

Collier's
November 17, 1906

Collier's
January 5, 1907

Collier's
April 24, 1909

Collier's
November 1, 1913

**Collier's
May 11, 1929**

**Collier's
October 24, 1936**

**Collier's
December 26, 1936**

Collier's

1888-1899	$16-22
1900-1929	$11-16
1930-1949	$6-11
1950-1959	$2-5
1960-	$1-3

    1901 Anniv. Issue, Xavier $65
    March 5, 1904, Christian $65
    Dec. 3, 1904, Parrish $65
    July 24, 1909, Parrish $55
    March 29, 1919, Norman Rockwell $32
    Jan. 25, 1929, Parrish $75
    December 28, 1929, All American Football Team . . . $22
    May 18, 1935, H.G. Wells $16
    February 17, 1951, Memoirs H. Hoover $11
    July 9, 1954, M. Monroe/Nixon $32
    November 11, 1955, Agatha Christie $22
    August 31, 1956 . . . . $11

Colorado Magazine

1923-1939	$3-6
1940-	$1-4

Comet

December 1940	$22
May 1941	$5

Comfort, 1930's $1-3

Confidential

1953-1961	$7-11

    May 1957, Marilyn $22
    Nov. 1957, Jayne Mansfield $22

Connoisseur

1901-1939	$7-11
1940-1959	$4-6
1960-	$2-4

Conservation Volunteer, 1940- $1-3

Consumer Bulletin
1931-1939 . . . . $2-4
1940- $2-3

Coronet
1937-1939 . . . . $3-6
1940-1959 . . . . $1-4
 July 1945, Eisenhower $9

Cosmopolitan
1886-1899 . . . . $11-16
1900-1929 . . . . $7-11
1930-1939 . . . . $4-6
1940-1949 . . . . $3-5
1950- $2-4
 May 1953, M. Monroe/Oklahoma $48

Country Gentleman
1883-1899 . . . . $11-22
1900-1919 . . . . $8-11
1920's $6-9
1930's $4-6
1940- $1-5
 Aug. 25, 1917, Norman Rockwell $44
 Sept. 8, 1917, Norman Rockwell $44
 April 1921, Rockwell $38
 August 1942, Blacks Picking Cotton $16
 February 1947, Disney $11

Country Life
Oct. 1926 . . . . $16
Dec. 1926 . . . . $16

Country Life In America, 1912- $3-5

Country Life, The New, 1901- $9-16

Country Man
1927-1939 . . . . $3-5
1940- $1-3

Craftsman, 1909 Fall $27

Crawdaddy
1967-1969 . . . . $27-37
1970 . . . . $22-32
1971. . . . . $16-22
1972 . . . . $16-22
1973-1979 . . . . $6-11
      1967 #1 . . . . $80
      1968 #19, Janis Joplin /Doors $80
      1970 #14, Jimi Hendrix $80

Creepy
#1. . . . . $27-46
#2. . . . . $13-24
#3-15. . . . . $8-13
All others. $3-10

Credit World
1912-1939 . . . . $2-4
1940- $1-2

Crow's Lumber Digest
1921-1939. . . . . $2-4
1940- $1-2

Cunkey's Home Journal, 1892- $2-5

Current History, July 1927 . . . . $11

Current Opinion, 1888-1925 . . . . $2-5

Dairy Goat Journal, 1940's $3-5

Dance, *1931, Alberto Varga* $55

Dare, *Aug.-Sept. 1956, Jayne Mansfield* $22

Daredevil Aces
July 1936. . . . . $44

Daredevil Aces (Continued)
December 1939. . . . . $32
January 1943. . . . . $22

Dearborn Independent, The
1900-1919 . . . . $2-5
1920 . . . . $1-3

Deep Sea Research
1953-1959 . . . . $5-10
1960- $2-5

Delaware History
1946-1959 . . . . $2-5
1960- $1-3

Delineator
1873-1899 . . . . $13-22
1900-1908 . . . . $10-15
1909-1919 . . . . $6-10
1920-1937 . . . . $4-6

Demorest's Monthly
1860's $22-32
1870's $16-27
1880's $11-22
1890's $6-11

Design
1899-1929 . . . . $6-11
1930-1949 . . . . $3-6
1950- $1-3

Dime Mystery Magazine
Oct. 1933 . . . . $110
Nov. 1934. . . . . $110
Jan. 1936 . . . . $110
1938-1949 . . . . $32-57

Disneyland Holiday, Summer 1957 . . . . $22

Display World
1923-1939 . . . . $3-5
1940- $1-3

Dog World
1916-1939 . . . . $5-10
1940- $1-4

Down Beat, *April 1, 1941, Dale Evans* $27

Dragnet Magazine, *Nov. 1928* $44

Ebony, 1952-1975 . . . . $3

Eerie
#1 . . . . $220
#2-3 . . . . $33-55
#4-50 . . . . $9-25
All others $5-10

Electrical Experimenter
1912-1920 . . . . $6-12
1921- $3-8

Electronics
1938-1957 . . . . $5
1958-1960 . . . . $3

Elvis in the Army Magazine, *Vol. 1 No. 1, 1959* $32

Entertainment, *June 1956, Jayne Mansfield* $27

Eros
    Spring 1962, Vol. 1 #1 . . . . $32
    Summer 1962, Vol. 1 #2 . . . . $48
    Fall 1962, Vol. 1 #3, Marilyn Monroe $67

Esquire
1930's $16-22
1940-1949 . . . . $11-16

Esquire (Continued)
1950-1960 . . . . $6-10
1970's $3-5

    October 1940, Alberto Varga $42
    June 1941, Varga $47
    Dec. 1945, Christmas issue $55
    Feb. 1946, Varga $55
    Sept. 1951, Marilyn Monroe $55
    Sept. 1952, Esther Williams $42
    Nov. 1955, Girl Fold Out $27

Etchings & Odysseys
No. 6 . . . . $16
No. 7 . . . . $22

Etude, The
1883-1899 . . . . $11-16
1900-1939 . . . . $5-10
1940's $2-6
1950's $1-4

Everybody's Magazine
1899-1929 . . . . $6-11

    December 1901, Parrish illustrations $42
    May 1903, Parrish illustration $42

Exciting Sports, 1st Issue 1941, Winter $10

Exciting Western, Nov. 1950 . . . . $22

Explorers Journal, 1921- $2-5

Eye
1950's $5-10
1960-1967 . . . . $3-5
    Special Issues will bring <u>much</u> higher prices !!!

Fame and Fortune Weekly, 1922-1927 . . . . $10-15

Family Circle
1932-1937 . . . . $6-12

Family Circle (Continued)
1938-1940's $4-8
1950's $3-6
1960's $2-5

Family Handyman, 1951- $1-3

Famous Fantastic Mysteries
1939 . . . . $42
1940's $10-20
1950-1953 . . . . $5-10

Famous Monsters of Filmland
#1, 1958 . . . . $220-330
#2 . . . . $160-220
#3 . . . . $110-160
#4 . . . . $110-160
#5-20 . . . . $55-110
#21-32 . . . . $27-55
All others $5-25

Famous Slugger Yearbook, 1967. . . . . $15

Fan, November 1957 . . . . $55

Fantastic
1950's $6-8
1960's $4-5
1970's $1-3
January 1968 . . . . $10
February 1970 . . . . $10

Fantastic Adventures
1939 . . . . $22-37
1940-1942 . . . . $10-20
1943-1949 . . . . $8-15
1950-1953 . . . . $5-10

Fantastic Story
1950-1954 . . . . $5-10

Fantasy & Science Fiction
1950 . . . . $16-27
1951-1959 . . . . $8-15
1960-1969 . . . . $5-8
1970's $3-5
1980's $1-3
    1949, Fall $55

Farm and Fireside
1877-1899 . . . . $4-10
1900-1957 . . . . $2-5

Farm and Stock, 1904- $2-5

Farm Journal, The
1891-1899 . . . . $5-10
1900- $2-6

Farm Life
1881-1899 . . . . $5-10
1900- $2-5

Farmers Review (Chicago), 1955 . . . . $5

Farmers Wife, The, 1912- $5-10
    June 1935, Dizzy Dean $22

Fashion Digest, 1937- $1-4

Fate
1940's $5-8
1950's $4-6
1960- $1-3

Fear!, July, 1960 . . . . $15

Field and Stream
1896-1919 . . . . $6-10
1920's $4-8
1930's $3-5
1940's $2-4
1950- $3-4

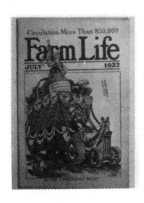

Front Page Detective, Oct. 1946 . . . . $5

Frontier Stories
1943-1949 . . . . $8-15
1950's $4-8

Fur Fish Game
1905-1939 . . . . $4-8
1940's $2-5
1950- $1-3

Future
1950's $3-5

G-Men
Nov. 1937. . . . . $10
Sept. 1942 . . . . $15

Gage, The, 1901- $10-15

Galaxy
1950's-1960's $4-7
1970's $2-3
           Oct. 1950 . . . . $15

Game Fowl News, 1925- $2-5

Genni – The Conjurers Magazine
1935-1949 . . . . $3-6
1950- $1-3

Gentleman Farmer Magazine, The, 1894- $4-10

Gentlewoman, The
1871-1929 . . . . $4-8
1930- $2-5

Gentry, *(Holiday Issue), 1952* $10

Ghost Stories
1927 . . . . $37-47
1928-1929 . . . . $27-37
1930's. $22-37

Glamour
1939-1940's $2-5
1950's $1-3

Glamour Photography, *Fall 1954, 1st Issue* $10

Glance Magazine, April 1950 . . . . $7
          May 1950, Marilyn "Norma Dougherty". $160

Gleason's Pictorial, 1851-1859 . . . . $22-37

Godey's Ladies Book, 1830-1898 . . . . $22-37

Golden Book, 1926-1935 . . . . $11-22

Golden Days, 1880-1907 . . . . $2-5

Golden Fleece, 1938-1939 . . . . $32-42

Golfing, 1933- $2-5

Good Health, July 1894 . . . . $12

Good Housekeeping
1855-1899 . . . . $5-10
1900-1919 . . . . $5-10
1920's $4-8
1930's $4-8
1940's $3-6
1950's $3-6
1960's $2-5
        July 1918, Jesse Wilcox Smith Cover $27

Good Stories, 1883- $3-8

Graphic, The, 1881- $11-27

Gray's Sporting Journal
1976-1989. . . . . $7
1990- $5

Great Hippie Hoax Magazine, The, 1968 . . . . $27

Green Book Album, The, 1908- $3-8

Grit and Steel
1898-1939 .... $5-10
1940- $1-4

Guatemala Today, Sept. 1936 .... $5

Gun Dog Magazine, 1981-1983 .... $8-11

Gun Report
June 1955 thru Dec. 1955 (Vol. #1-#6) $15
1956- $3

Guns & Ammo, 1958-1959 .... $2-5

Gun World Magazine, 1960- $3

Handloader
Vol. #1-#100 .... $3
#101- $2

Happy Hour Magazine, 1905 .... $11

Hardboiled
#11-14 .... $11-16

Harper's Bazar
1867-1899 .... $10-15
1900-1919 .... $8-12
1920's $6-10
1930's $4-8
1940's $3-5
1950's- $1-3
    July 1871 .... $22
    June 1872 .... $22
    Dec. 1895, Parrish $140

Harper's Monthly
1850-1899 .... $6-11
1900-1919 .... $4-8
1920's $3-6

Harper's Monthly (Continued)
1930's $2-4
1940's- $1-3

Harper's Weekly
1857-1860 .... $11-16
1861-1865 .... $16-22
1866-1899 .... $5-10
1900-1916 .... $4-8
   July 24, 1858, Hudson Bay Gold Fields $37
   Sept. 1901, McKinley $22

Harpoon Magazine, *Sept. 1974, 1st Issue* $22

Hearst's
1901-1925 .... $11-22
1925- $5-10

Hearst's Cosmopolitan, 1934 .... $10-12

Hearth and Home, 1868-1875 .... $5-15

Help!, Aug. 1960, 1st Issue $8

High, 1958-1959 .... $5-10

Hi-Life, *March 1958, 1st Issue* $10

Hi-Teen, *August 1962, 1st Issue* $10

Hobbies
1931-1949 .... $3-6
1950's $2-4
1960's- $1-3

Hockey News, 1947- $1-4

Holiday Magazine
1946-1949 .... $6-10
1950's $3-5
1960's $2-4

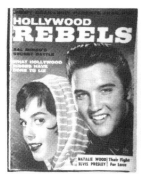  

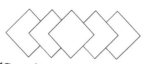

Holiday Magazine (Continued)

Vol. 1 No. 1, March 1946 .... $22
Vol. 1 No. 2, April 1946, Carousel $15

Holland's Magazine

1925-1926 .... $5-7
1930's $4-6
1940's $3-5

Hollywood

1911-1919 .... $22-32
1920-1942 .... $16-22

Sept. 1933, Mae West $32
Feb. 1934, Norma Shearer. $27
Nov. 1935, Carole Lombard $27
April 1936, Gloria Stuart. $27
May 1938, 7 Dwarfs $65
March 1937, Jean Harlow $27
Dec. 1937, Gary Cooper & Sigrid Gurie $27
March 1939, Deanna Durbin, Errol Flynn $27
May 1940, Cary Grant $32
Oct. 1940, Mickey Rooney & Judy Garland $32
Nov. 1940, Ida Lupino $27
Jan. 1941, Gary Cooper $27
Nov. 1941, Dorothy Lamour $27

Hollywood Dream Girl

1955, 1st Edition, Marilyn Monroe $32

Hollywood Life Stories

#4 1954, Ann Blyth $15
#8 1958, Liz Taylor $22
#10 1960, Liz Taylor $12

Hollywood Reporter

1930's $11-22
1940's $8-15
1950's $3-6

Hollywood Romances, *#9 1956, Kim Novak* $15

Hollywood Secrets Annual, #4 *Edd Byrnes, S. Dee* $10

Hollywood Stars
    June 1956, Grace Kelly, Shirley Jones, etc. $15
    May 1958, Rock Hudson, Elvis $10

Hollywood's Family Album
    #2 March 1949, Dennis Morgan $22

Hollywood Yearbook
    #1 1950, June Allyson $15
    #4 1953, Liz Taylor $22

Home Arts Magazine, 1937-1940 . . . . $3-5
    May 1935, Maud Toussey Fangell $10

Home Magazine, The, 1888-1908 . . . . $3-8

Homemaker, The, 1897- $2-6

Homestead, The, 1855- $3-10

Home Workshop, 1946. . . . . $3

Hoof Beats, 1933- $2-5

Hoofs and Horns, 1930- $2-5

Horizon Magazine
    Sept. 1961, Andrew Wyeth $10
    Summer 1975, Erte cover $5

Horror Stories
October 1935 . . . . $77
June/July 1938 . . . . $67
December 1940 . . . . $57

Horseman, The
1877-1899. . . . . $10-15
1900-1919. . . . . $8-12
1920-1939. . . . . $6-10

Horseman, The (Continued)
1940-1959. . . . . $2-6
1960-. $1-3

Hot Rod
1950's $5
1960's $3
1970 . . . . $2

Hounds & Hunting, 1922 . . . . $5-10

Household Family Magazine
1950's $5-10

House Beautiful
1896-1919. . . . . $11-16
1920's $8-12
1930's $6-10
1940's $3-5
1950's $2-4
1960- $1-3
    Oct. 1959, Frank Lloyd Wright $10

House & Garden
1901-1919. . . . . $8-12
1920's $6-10
1930's $5-9
1940's $4-8
1950- $1-3

Household Ledger, The
1844-1849. . . . . $11-16
1850-1899. . . . . $5-10
1900- $2-6

Household Magazine, The, 1900- $2-5

Housewife, The
1882-1899. . . . . $7-10
1900-1917 . . . . $4-7

Hullabaloo Magazine
6-1967, Hermans Hermits $30

Humbug
1957-1958 . . . . $5-10

Hunter, Trader, Trapper
1864-1899. . . . . $16-22
1900-1919. . . . . $11-16
1920-1939 . . . . $5-10

Hush-Hush, May 1955 . . . . $10

If
1952-1970 . . . . $4-10
  March 1952 . . . . $15
  October 1955 . . . . $15

Illustrated Companion, The, 1871- $2-5

Illustrated Graphic News, The, 1880- $10-20

Illustrated London News, The
1842-1849. . . . . $22-32
1850-1899. . . . . $16-22
1900-1939. . . . . $10-15
1940-1949 . . . . $8-10
1950- $4-7

Illustrated Sporting and Dramatic News, The
1874-1879. . . . . $22-32
1880-1899. . . . . $16-22
1900-1939. . . . . $10-15
1940-1949 . . . . $8-10
1950- $4-7

Illustrated War News, *Spanish American War 1898* . . . $55-110

Imagination
1950's $3-10
  October 1950 (#1) $22

Ladies Home Journal
June 1901

Ladies Home Journal
September 1904

Ladies Home Journal
January 1909

Ladies Home Journal - July 1912

Ladies Home Journal - May 1913

Ladies Home Journal
April 1921

Ladies Home Journal
January 1931

Judge (Continued)
1940's $5-10
      May 1935 . . . . $27

Kluxer, The, 1924- $11-22

Ladies Home Journal
1883-1899 . . . . $16-22
1900's $10-15
1910's $10-15
1920's $8-12
1930's $5-10
1940's. $3-6
1950's $2-5
      Dec. 1912, Parrish Cover $75
      Nov. 1924, Wyeth Illus. $20
      June 1930, Parrish Cover $40
      July 1941, Bette Davis $15

Ladies World
1886-1899 . . . . $11-22
1900-1918 . . . . $8-15

Lady's Circle
      Dec. 1968, Lucille Ball & Childern $10

Laff
1940's $6-10
1950's $3-7

Landscape Architecture, Oct. 1912 . . . . $10

Laugh Book
      Dec. 1959, Kim Novak $6

Leslie's Weekly
1855-1899 . . . . $16-27
1900's $13-22
1910's $10-15
1920-1922 . . . . $8-12

Leslie's Weekly (Continued)

September 2, 1915 . . . . $37
Oct. 5, 1916, Norman Rockwell $32
March 30, 1918 , Rockwell $32
The War in Pictures Issues , 1918 . . . . $55
March 22, 1919, Norman Rockwell $37

Liberty Magazine

1924-1939 . . . . $5-15
1940's $4-6
March 7, 1936, Clark Gable $27
February 12, 1938, Disney's Snow White $22
October 25, 1941, Hitler $22

Life Magazine

1883-1936 . . . . $10-15
1937-1949 . . . . $5-10
1950- $2-8
May 10, 1917, Rockwell cover $42
Dec. 1922, Maxfield Parrish $65
Nov. 23, 1936, Ft. Peck Dam $55
Nov. 30, 1936, West Point Cadet $42
Dec. 7, 1936, Skiing $32
Dec. 14, 1936, Archbishop of Canterbury $27
Dec. 28, 1936, Metro Opera Ballet $22
Jan. 4, 1937, Franklin D. Roosevelt $15
May 3, 1937, Jean Harlow. $55
May 17, 1937, Dionne Quintuplets $32
Sept. 6, 1937, Harpo Marx $32
November 8, 1937, Greta Garbo $37
Dec. 13, 1937, Locomotive $15
Feb. 7, 1938, Gary Cooper $22
May 23, 1938, Errol Flynn $27
June 20, 1938, Rudolph Valentino $37
July 11, 1938, Shirley Temple $42
Aug. 22, 1938, Astaire & Rogers $37
Oct. 17, 1938, Carole Lombard $32
Dec. 19, 1938, Mary Martin $22
Jan. 23, 1939, Bette Davis $37
March 13, 1939, World's Fair Sculpture $27

Life Magazine (Continued)

May 1, 1939, Joe DiMaggio $47

May 22, 1939, World's Fair Guide $32

Sept. 11, 1939, Benito Mussolini $22

Dec. 11, 1939, Betty Grable $27

Jan. 29, 1940, Lana Turner $22

July 15, 1940, Rita Hayworth $22

Sept. 2, 1940, Dionne Quintuplets $22

Dec. 9, 1940, Ginger Rogers $27

Jan. 6, 1941, Katherine Hepburn $32

Aug. 11, 1941, Rita Hayworth $22

Sept. 1, 1941, Ted Williams $27

Oct. 13, 1941, Turner & Gable $32

Dec. 8, 1941, Commander of Far East $15

March 2, 1942, Ginger Rogers $32

March 30, 1942, Shirley Temple Grows Up $42

June 1, 1942, Hedy Lamarr $27

Jan. 18, 1943, Rita Hayworth $22

July 12, 1943, Roy Rogers & Trigger $37

July 19, 1943, Air Force Pilot (WASP) $15

Oct. 16, 1944, Bacall $27

Dec. 11, 1944, Judy Garland $32

April 23, 1945, Harry S. Truman $22

July 16, 1945, Audie Murphy $22

Sept. 17, 1945, Gen. D. MacArthur $22

Sept. 24, 1945, Col. Jimmy Stewart $27

Nov. 12, 1945, Ingrid Bergman $15

Dec. 3, 1945, Spencer Tracy $15

Feb. 4, 1946, B. Hope & B. Crosby $15

July 29, 1946, Vivian Leigh $22

Nov. 25, 1946, Baby/10th Anniversary $27

Dec. 2, 1946, Ingrid Bergman $22

July 14, 1947, Elizabeth Taylor $32

Dec. 6, 1948, Montgomery Cliff $27

Aug. 1, 1949, Joe DiMaggio $32

May 8, 1950, Jackie Robinson. $42

June 12, 1950, Hopalong Cassidy $32

April 7, 1952, Marilyn Monroe $67

April 6, 1953, Luci, Desi & Family $27

April 20, 1953, Marlon Brando $22

Life Magazine (Continued)

May 25, 1953, M. Monroe/J. Russell. $42
June 8, 1953, Roy Campanella. $24
July 20, 1953, John & Jackie Kennedy $27
April 26, 1954, Grace Kelly. $22
Sept. 13, 1954, Judy Garland $27
Jan. 10, 1955, Greta Garbo $15
Oct. 3, 1955, Rock Hudson $27
June 25, 1956, Mickey Mantle. $42
April 15, 1957, ErnieKovacks $15
April 28, 1958, Willie Mays $27
Dec. 1, 1958, Ricky Nelson $27
April 20, 1959, Marilyn Monroe $32
Nov. 9, 1959, Marilyn Monroe $32
Aug. 15, 1960, M. Monroe & Yves Montand $27
Dec. 19, 1960, Kennedy's sons Christening $15
Dec. 26, 1960, Xmas Spec. Dbl. Issue $22
July 28, 1961, Brigitte Bardot $15
Aug. 18, 1961, Mantle/Maris $37
April 13, 1962, Burton/Taylor $42
June 22, 1962, M. Monroe $32
Aug. 17, 1962, Memories of Marilyn $32
Sept. 28, 1962, Don Drysdale $22
Aug. 2, 1963, Sandy Koufax $27
Nov. 29, 1963, JFK Assassination $22
Dec. 13, 1963, JFK Memorial Edition $10
March 6, 1964, Cassius Clay $22
Aug. 28, 1964, Beatles $32
May 7, 1965, John Wayne/Cancer $22
July 30, 1965, M. Mantle $22
Jan. 7, 1966, Sean Connery as 007 . . . . $22
March 11, 1966, Batman on cover $27
Sept. 8, 1967, Carl Yastrzemski $27
Sept. 13, 1968, The Beatles $27
Sept. 21, 1969, Woodstock Special Ed $37
Oct. 15, 1971, Opening of Disney World $27
March 24, 1972, Chamberlin & Abdul Jabbar $15
November 1978, Mickey's 50th Birthday $27

Light, 1887- $22-42

Lions Roar, The, 1941- $22-44

Literary Digest
1890-1907 . . . .$10-15
1908-1919 . . . .$8-12
1920's $3-8
1930-1938 . . . .$3-5
  Mar. 6, 1909, Mucha Cover $47
  Dec. 4, 1909, Mucha Cover $42
  July 1910, Mucha Cover $27
  Feb. 8, 1919, Rockwell $32
  July 24, 1922, Rockwell $27
  Sept. 4, 1920, Rockwell $27
  Dec. 22, 1923 . . . . $32

Literary Review, 1957- $1-3

Lithographers Journal
1915-1939 . . . .$4-10
1940- $1-4

London Mystery Magazine, *Vol. 1 No. 1* $40

Lone Scout, The, 1915- $5-15

Look
1937-1939 . . . . $10-15
1940's $6-12
1950's $4-8
1960's $3-6
1970-1972 . . . . $2-4
  May 11, 1937, Mae West $45
  Nov. 23, 1937, Joan Crawford $55
  July 19, 1938, Marlene Dietrich $55
  July 18, 1939, Vivian Leigh $20
  December 5, 1939, Vera Zorina $20
  Feb. 13, 1940, Terry & The Pirates $32
  Feb. 27, 1940, Superman vs Hitler $55
  May 7, 1940, Judy Garland & Mickey Rooney $20
  October 8, 1940, Garland/Rooney $20

Look (Continued)

December 3, 1940, Don Winslow. $27
October 20, 1942, Flash Gordon, Vol. 6 #21. . . . . $15
April 26, 1949, Joe DeMaggio & Joe Jr. $44
June 21, 1949, Ingrid Bergman $15
July 18, 1950, Flying Saucers/Yankee's $15
August 29, 1950, Hopalong Cassidy $32
April 21, 1953, Lucy, Desi & Family $15
Nov. 13, 1956, Elvis. $55
April 15, 1958, Elvis $55
July 5, 1960, Marilyn Monroe. $20
Jan. 31, 1961, Marilyn Monroe. $20
Nov. 17, 1964, JFK Memorial $27
April 6, 1971, Walt Disney World Opening. $15

Lot-Bottle News, 1976-1979 . . . . $2

Louisiana Conservationist, 1948- $2-5

Lowdown, *January 1961, Zsa Zsa Gabor* $10

Madame Magazine

July 1904 . . . . $27
August 1904. . . . . $27

Mademoiselle, *Dec. 1941, Alberto Varga* $10

Mad Magazine *(Issues #1-23 were Comic Books)*

#1. . . . . $1,500-3,000
#2-23 . . . . $200-500
#24. . . . . $200-400
#25-30. . . . . $100-150
#31-50. . . . . $30-90
#51-80. . . . . $15-25
#81-170. . . . . $5-15
#171-. $2-5

Magazine Digest

1950's $3-6

Mans, 1964-1966. . . . . $3

Mans Illustrated, March 1965. . . . . $3

Mans Peril, Nov. 1966. . . . . $3

Mans World, 1964-1965. . . . . $3

Master Detective, *April 1934, Dillinger* $20

McCall's
1873-1899 . . . . $16-22
1900-1919. . . . . $10-15
1920-1939 . . . . $6-10
1940-1949 . . . . $3-5
1950- $1-3
    April 1921, Paper Dolls $20
    December 1921, Paper Dolls $20
    August 1922, Paper Dolls $20
    April 1926. Paper Dolls $20
    August 1932, Mickey Mouse's Father $32

McClure's Magazine
1893-1899 . . . . $5-10
1900-1929 . . . . $3-8
    Jan.-1905, Parrish Cover $27
    Oct. 1906, Parrish Cover $22

Mechanics, 1882- $10-15

Mechanix Illustrated
    1928-1939 . . . . $4-10
    1940-1959. . . . . $3-6
    1960-. $1-3

Melody, *July 1935, Crosby* $6

Mentor, The
1913-1930 . . . . $6-12
    March 1922, Arabian Nights, Parrish $25

Metal Worker, The, 1857-1889 . . . . $10-20

Metropolitan Magazine
1895-1899 .... $22-27
1900-1924 .... $5-15

Mickey Mouse Magazine
Vol. 1 #1, 1935 .... $160
Vol. 1 #12, Sept. 1936 .... $60

Mid Week Pictorial, June 20, 1931 .... $25

Mining & Metallurgy, Sept. 1939 .... $5

Mr. America, *1st Issue - Jan. 1958* $22

Mr. Foster's Travel Magazine, 1914 .... $15

Mobsters, February 1953 .... $20

Model Airplane News, June 1940 .... $15

Model Railroader
1934-1939 .... $4-8
1940-1949 .... $3-6
1950- $1-3

Modern Man
March 1955, Marilyn Monroe $65
April 1956, Jayne Mansfield $27
June 1956, Marilyn Monroe $65
March 1961, Jayne Mansfield $32
1966, Jayne Mansfield $17

Modern Brewery Age
1923-1939 .... $3-5
1940- $1-3

Modern Homemaking, 1890- $2-5

Modern Miller, 1876-1892 .... $10-20

Modern Photography, *1954, M. Monroe Cover* $47

Modern Priscilla
1887-1899 . . . . : $8-15
1900's $6-12
1910's $5-10
1920-1930 . . . . $3-8

Modern Romances, 1940-1950's $2-5

Modern Screen
1930's $16-27
1940's $10-15
1950's $5-10
1960's $2-5
   Sept. 1931, Nancy Carroll $32
   March 1934, Miriam Hopkins $32
   January 1935, Anna Sten by Christy $32
   December 1935, Claudette Colbert by Christy $32
   December 1936, Merle Oberon $32
   January 1938, Katherine Hepburn $44
   May 1938, Carole Lombard $44
   July 1938, Simone Simon $37
   October 1938, Irene Dunne by Christy $32
   December 1938, Alice Faye $37
   January 1939, Shirley Temple X-Mas cvr $37
   April 1939, Deanna Durbin $37
   February 1940, Judy Garland & Mickey Rooney . . . $37
   September 1940, Claudette Colbert $27
   April 1941, Olivia DeHavilland $27
   May 1941, Barbara Stanwyck $27
   October 1943, Betty Grable $27
   November 1943, Errol Flynn $27
   April 1944, Shirley Temple $27
   May 1944, Deanna Durbin $22
   September 1944, Frank Sinatra $22
   August 1947, Comel Wilde $22
   February 1948, Shirley Temple $22
   April 1948, Esther Williams $22
   September 1951, Elizabeth Taylor $22
   July 1952, Rita Hayworth $22
   November 1952, Jane Powell $22

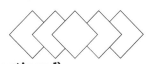

Modern Screen (Continued)
February 1953, Liz Taylor $22
April 1953, Doris Day $22
April 1954, L. Taylor, M. Monroe's Honeymoon $22
June 1958, Debbie Reynolds $16
September 1958, D. Reynolds/E. Fisher $12
September 1959, Liz Taylor/Eddie Fisher $12
May 1968, Mia Farrow $10
July 1968, Lennon Sisters $10

Modern Teen
August 1957, Elvis $80

Modern Thinker, March 1932, 1st Issue $10

Modern Woman, 1897- $3-10

Monsterland, #3, June 1985, Godzilla $10

Monster Parade, 1958-1959 . . . . $27-33

Monsters and Things
January 1959, #1 - Rodan, Frankenstein $27
April 1959, #2 – The Frankenstein Legend $22

Monster World
#1, November 1964, Lionel Atwill $27
#2, January 1965, The Munsters $22

Mothers Magazine, The, 1905- $5-10

Motion Picture
1910-1939 . . . . $27-44
1940-1959 . . . . $22-32
1960-1969 . . . . $10-20
1970- $5-10
March 1917, Violet Mersereau $47
May 1917, Anita Stewart $47
April 1931, Marlene Dietrich $47
June 1935, Marlene Dietrich $47

Motion Picture (Continued)

July 1935, Jean Harlow. $55
March 1936, Shirley Temple $55
April 1936, Bette Davis $47
May 1936, Jean Harlow $55
Nov. 1936, Ginger Rogers $55
Dec. 1936, Joan Crawford $47
July 1937, Marlene Dietrich $55
Feb. 1938, Katherine Hepburn $47
March 1946, Shirley Temple $37

Motion Picture Classic

March 1926, Greta Nissen $25
September 1926, Claire Windsor $25
April 1931, Clara Bow $40
June 1931, Anita Page $32

Motion Picture Herald

1906-1929 . . . . $27-44
1930-1939 . . . . $22-32
1940-1949 . . . . $10-20
1950-1969 . . . . $5-10
1970- $2-5

Motor, Jan. 1927 . . . . $27

Motor Age

April 28, 1904 . . . . $15
February 24, 1910 . . . . $15

Motor Life, 1955-1961 . . . . $3

Motorcycling & Bicycling, 1920's $27

Motor Sport, 1955-1956 . . . . $3

Motor Thrife, 1957-1959 . . . . $3

Motor Trend, 1955-1967 . . . . $3

Movie Classic

1933 . . . . $22-44
1934 . . . . $22-44

Movie Fan

Movie Greats, 1971 . . . . $7

Movieland

Movie Life

Movie Life Yearbook

Movie Mirror

Movie Mirror (Continued)
December 1931, Jean Harlow $90
December 1936, Shirley Temple $85
May 1938, Dopey of Snow White $85
May 1959, Elvis. $77
May 1968, Elvis $27

Movie Play
1946-1949 . . . . $10-20
1950's $7-15

Movie Radio
1931-1939 . . . . $15-20
1940-1943 . . . . $15-20
Jan. 24, 1942, Gene Autry $30

Movies
1930's-1940's $10-15
1950's $5-10
October 1933, Ruby Keeler $32
February 1942, Ann Sheridan $25
September 1943, Ingrid Bergman $32
December 1944, Ella Raines $25
May 1945, Shirley Temple $25
April 1956, Grace Kelly $25

Movie Screen Yearbook
#1, Debbie Reynolds $20
#8, Connie Stevens $10
#19, Liz & Burton $10

Movie Show
1940's $5-15
December 1944, Ann Sheridan $20
March 1946, Rita Hayworth $25
April 1946, Dorothy McGuire $25
December 1946, June Allyson $25
February 1947, Linda Darnell $25
November 1947, Lana Turner $25

Movie Spotlight, February 1953 . . . . $15

Movie Stars, *August 1978, Elvis.* $12

Movie Stars Parade
1940's $15-25
1950-1956 . . . . $5-15
        Fall 1940, Spencer Tracy, Hedy Lamarr, etc. $32
        May 1950, June Allyson $16
        April 1961, Elvis $44

Movie Story
1937-1939 . . . . $27-44
1940-1950 . . . . $20-30
        August 1939, Wizard of Oz $77
        September 1940, Garland/Rooney $55
        December 1941, Betty Grable $40
        February 1942, Lana Turner $40
        May 1942, J. Wayne/M. Dietrich $40

Movie Teen Illustrated
1957-1968 . . . . $10-20
        Fall 1957, Jimmie Dean $32
        October 1960, Elvis $32
        Summer 1962, American Bandstand $25
        December 1962, Elvis $25
        April 1963, Elvis/Bandstand $25
        November 1963, Darren/Elvis, Nelson's Wed $25
        January 1964, Elvis/Dion $25
        May 1964, Elvis/Beatles $25
        July 1967, Stones/Beatles/Cher $25
        October 1967, Priscilla/Beatles/Grateful Dead $25
        February 1968, Jimi Hendrix. $25
        April 1968, Janis Joplin/Sonny & Cher $25
        July 1968, Cream $25
        October 1968, Elvis/Beatles/Box Tops etc. $25

Movie Time
        August 1954 , Esther Williams $12
        October 1954, Lana Turner $15
        April 1955, June Allyson $10

Movie TV Secrets, 1963-1968 . . . . $4-10
        Vol. 1 No. 6, 1959, Elvis $25

Movie World
1966-1972 . . . . $5-10

Movie World (Continued)

    November 1958, Ricky and David, Elvis,
        D. Reynolds, D. Clark $20
    May 1959, Elvis $37

Moving Picture Stories, 1920's $7-10

Munsey, The, 1889-1929 .... $3-6
    February 1899, article about Klondike $10

Munyon's Illustrated World, 1885- $10-20

Munyon's Magazine, 1901 .... $12

National Builder, The, 1914 .... $5

National Food Magazine, July 1911 .... $7

National Geographic Magazine, The

    1888 Vol. 1 No. 1 .... $5,000+
    1888-1889, Vol. 1 No.'s 2,3,4 .... $3,000+
1890-1895 .... $300-500
1896-1899 .... $100-200
1900-1905 .... $100-150
1906-1909 .... $25-50
1910's $10-20
1920's $5-10
1930's $4-6
1940's $2-5
1950- $1-3

National Life Magazine

1920's $3-5
    1928, Hoover $10

National Magazine, The, 1880- $4-8

National Monthly, The, 1909 .... $3-6

National Lampoon Gentlemen's Bathroom Companion

1975 .... $10

National Sportsman
1900-1919. . . . . $10
1920-1929. . . . . $7
1930-1941. . . . . $5

National Stockman and Farmer, The, 1876- $3-6

Natural History
1900's $5-10
1910-1939 . . . . $4-8
1940- . . . . : $2-5

Nature Magazine, 1914-1941. . . . . $4-10

Nebraska Educational Journal, *Oct. 1928, Parrish* $50

Needlecraft
1909-1919 . . . . $10-15
1920's $8-12
1930-1940. . . . . $4-8

New Century, The, Nov. 30, 1902 . . . . $6

New Idea Woman's Magazine
1901. . . . . $35
1902 . . . . $27

New Movie
1930's. $16-27
     November 1930, Maureen O'Sullivan $70
     Feb. 1934, Katherine Hepburn $44

New Movie Album, The, *1930, Greta Garbo* $55-80

New Stars Over Hollywood
1940's. $5-10
     1945, Mary Anderson, June Allyson, etc. $20

Newsweek
1925-1929 . . . . $5-10
1930's $4-8
1940's $3-6
1950's $2-4
1960- $1-3

Newsweek (Continued)

> *October 4, 1937, Hitler & Mussolini* $27
> *May 29, 1944, Dionne Quintuplet s* $15
> *Feb. 24, 1964, Beatles.* $20
> *Oct. 16, 1972, M. Monroe* $27

New Worlds, 1953-1958. . . . . $3-5

New Yorker, The, Feb. 23, 1957 . . . . $10

New York Illustrated News, The, 1887- $10-20

New York Lumber Trade Journal, The

1883-1909 . . . . $16-27
1910's $10-15
1920's $8-10
1930's $5-8
1940's $2-5
1950's- $1-3

Night and Day, 1949-1954 . . . . $10-15

North American DeCoy Magazine

1967, July, Aug., Sep. $32
1967, Oct., Nov., Dec. $27
1968-1971 . . . . $20
1972. . . . . $15
1973, Winter & Spring. $10
1973, Summer & Fall. $17
1974, Winter & Fall. $10
1974, Spring & Summer. $17
1975, Winter & Summer. $4-8
1975, Spring & Fall. $15
1976 . . . . $10
1976, Winter & Summer & Fall. $15
1977. . . . . $4
1978 . . . . $4
1978, Spring. $10
1979 . . . . $4
Not issued in 1980
1981-1984. . . . . $7

Northern Pacific, 1901 . . . . $27

Northwest Magazine, The
1882-1899 . . . . $10-15
1900-1909 . . . . $6-12
1910-1939 . . . . $5-10
1940- $2-5

Northwestern Agriculturist, The,
1885-1899 . . . . $5-10
1900- $3-5

Nostalgia Illustrated, 1975 . . . . $4-8

Official Detective Stories, Jan. 1943. . . . . $12

Ohio Magazine, 1989 . . . . $4-5

Ohio Practical, The
1848-1899 . . . . $3-10
1900- $1-5

Old Bottle, 1968- $2-4

Oliver Optics Magazine, 1867- $5-10

Orange-Judd Farmer, The
1842-1899. . . . . $5-10
1900-. $2-6

Oriental Rug Magazine
1928-1939 . . . . $3-6
1940- $1-4

Our Little Grangers, 1879- $3-10

Outdoor American, Oct. 1926 . . . . $6

Outdoor Life
1897-1899 . . . . $8-12
1900's $6-10
1910's $4-8
1920's $3-6
1930's- $2-5
1940- $1-4

Outing Magazine
1882-1899 . . . . $16-27
1900's $10-20
1910's $6-12
1920-1923 . . . . $5-10

Outlook
1870-1899 . . . . $5-10
1900-1935 . . . . $2-5

Pacific Monthly, The, Feb. 1911 . . . . $10

Pageant, *June 1946, Norma Jean* $44

Palm Beach Life, Feb. 17, 1931 . . . . $6

Parents Magazine, November 1949 . . . . $5

Pathfinder
1940's $3-5
        April 20, 1949, Lou Boudreau $10
        April 23, 1952, Bill Veeck $10

Pearsons Magazines, 1901-1902 . . . . $2

Peek
1938-1941 . . . . $5-10
        January 1938, 1st Issue $25

Penthouse Magazine
1969 . . . . $15-30
1970-1979 . . . . $5-10
1980- $2-5
        March 1976, P. Barnes $20
        Feb. 1980, D. Harry $20
        Sept. 1984, V. Williams & T. Lords $32
        Nov. 1984. V. Williams. $20
        Sept. 1985, Madonna $32
        June 1987, S. Fox $25
        Sept. 1987, Madonna $20

People Magazine
1974 . . . . $5-10
1975 . . . . $3-6
1980's $1-5

People Magazine (Contined)

    Jan. 13, 1975, Elvis $15

    Feb. 10. 1975, Cher $15

People's Home Journal

1885-1899 . . . . $10-15

1900- $3-10

People's Popular Monthly

    May 1917, Rockwell $65

    June 1917, Rockwell $65

    May 15, 1920, Rockwell $44

    Aug. 1923, Rockwell $44

Personal Story, *June 1955, 1st issue, Lollobrigida* $10

Peterson's Magazine, 1842-1898. . . . . $15-33

Photo Exhibit, July 1957 . . . . $8

Photography Magazine

1950's $3-10

    August 1954, Marilyn Monroe $50

Photoplay

1911-1939. . . . . $15-30

1940-1959 . . . . $5-15

1960-1979 . . . . $3-8

May 1980, Last issue (became US) $10

    January 1914, Mary Pickford, Owen Moore $44

    Sept. 1914, Mary Pickford $44

    June 1919, Constance Talmadge $35

    Nov. 1919, Lilian Gish $45

    October 1920, Mary Pickford $35

    April 1922, Dorothy Gish $35

    June 1924, Leatrice Joy $35

    Sept. 1924, Colleen Moore $35

    November 1924, Jackie Coogan $35

    Feb. 1925, Florence Vidor $35

    April 1925, May Allison $35

    May 1925, Norma Shearer $36

    March 1926, Gilda Gray $35

    Nov. 1926, Renee Adoree $35

    July 1927, Norma Talmadge $35

    Nov. 1927, Jette Goudal $33

Photoplay (Continued)

Sept. 1928, Gloria Swanson $35
Dec. 1928, Janet Gaynor $35
April 1929, Clara Bow. $35
May 1929, June Collyer $35
Aug. 1929, Greta Garbo $44
Dec. 1929, Norma Talmadge $35
March 1930, Joan Crawford $35
July 1930, Jeanette MacDonald by Christy $35
Aug. 1930, Greta Garbo $55
May 1931, Marlene Dietrich $44
Aug. 1932, Jean Harlow $35
November 1933, Marlene Dietrich $35
June 1934, Carole Lombard $45
May, 1935, Jean Harlow $35
Aug. 1935, Kay Francis $35
Nov. 1935, Carole Lombard $35
April 1936, Joan Crawford $35
Dec. 1936, Shirley Temple. $35
March 1937, Jean Harlow. $44
May 1937, J. Harlow/R. Taylor $44
June 1937, Shirley Temple. $44
Aug. 1937, Claudette Colbert $45
Nov. 1937, Shirley Temple $44
Jan. 1938, Irene Dunne $35
May 1938, Shirley Temple $35
July 1938, Clark Gable $35
October 1938, Bette Davis $35
November 1938, Deanna Durbin $35
December 1938, Tyrone Power $44
December 1939, Myrna Loy $35
October 1940, Claudette Colbert $25
November 1940, Paulette Goddard $25
December 1940, Judy Garland $25
August 1941, Judy Garland $25
March 1942, Bette Davis $25
July 1943, Judy Garland $25
April 1949, Betty Grable $25
Feb. 1953, Marilyn Monroe $35
December 1953, Marilyn Monroe $30
October 1956, Elvis $50
July 1957, Elvis $50
October 1958, Elvis $35
March 1960, Elvis $25
November 1974, Elvis $15

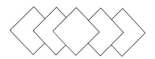

Photoplay Tribute, 1977, Elvis $20

Phrenological Journal, 1821- $10-25

Physical Culture
1903- $5-15

PIC
1938-1947 . . . . $5-10
    August 9, 1938, Carole Lombard $15
    Dec. 26, 1939, D. Lamour & R. Preston $15
    Sept. 16, 1941, Veronica Lake $15
    Jan. 6, 1942, Gene Tierney $15
    Oct. 24, 1944, Lucille Ball $22
    Jan. 30, 1945, Deanna Durbin & Jerome Kern $22
Pic Quarterly Baseball, Spring 1949 . . . . $15

Pictorial Review Embroidery Magazine
1909- $5-15
    July 1922 . . . . $25
    June 1924 . . . . $20

Picture Magazine, *Feb. 1938, 1st Issue.* $27

Picturegoer
1946-1949 . . . . $5-10
1950's $4-6
    September 6, 1952, Roy Rogers $15
    June 11, 1955, Piper Laurie $15
    June 21, 1958, Joanna Moore $10
    May 2, 1959, Gordon Scott $10
    December 12, 1959, Brigitte Bardot $15

Picture Play
1916-1919 . . . . $27-40
1920's $22-33
1930's $10-20
    November 1932, Marlene Dietrich $55
    November 1933, Greta Garbo $55
    May 1934, Katharine Hepburn $55
    May 1936, Ginger Rogers $25
    June 1936, Claudette Colbert $25
    July 1936, Madge Evans $25
    September 1936, Miriam Hopkins $25
    October 1936, Greta Garbo $25

Picture Show
> *October 1947, Esther Williams* $10
> *January 1949, Myrna Dell.* $8
> *March 1951, Li'l Abner* $6

Picture World
> *Sept. 1942, 1st Issue* $8

Pictorial Review
1899-1909 . . . . $20-27
1910-1929 . . . . $15-20
1930-1939 . . . . $10-15

Pilgrim, The, 1900- $3-6

Planter and Stockman, 1885- $3-6

Planet, 1940-1950 . . . . $10-20

Playboy
1953, Dec. #1, M. Monroe $1,500
1954 . . . . $150-250
1955-1959 . . . . $25-55
1960-1969 . . . . $15-33
1970- $3-10
> *January 1954* $1000
> *Feb. 1954* $700
> *Feb. 1955* $100
> *Sept. 1955* $75-100

Police Gazette
1948-1949 . . . . $15-20
1950's $9-12
1960's $5-8
> *Nov. 1955, MacArthur* $25

Popular Aviation Magazine
Sept. & Oct. 1935 . . . . $33

Popular Hit Songs, *May 1947, Betty Grable* $10

Popular Mechanics
1902-1909 . . . . $5-10

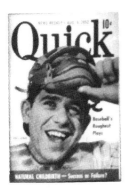
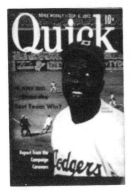

Popular Mechanics (Continued)
1910-1939 . . . . $4-8
1940-1959 . . . . $3-6
1960- $1-3

Popular Photography, *Oct. 1956, Kim Novak* $5

Popular Science Monthly
1872-1899 . . . . $10-20
1900-1939 . . . . $8-15
1940-1959 . . . . $4-10
1960- $1-5

Popular Screen, Sept. 1934 . . . . $30

Popular Songs, 1930's $4-8

Practical Builder Magazine, 1952 . . . . $2-4

Practical Farmer, 1895-1897 . . . . $5-10

Prairie Farmer, The
1841-1899 . . . . $5-10
1900-1939 . . . . $4-8
1940-1959 . . . . $3-6
1960- $1-3
    January 11, 1941, Centennial $15

Printing Art
    January 1913, Frank X. Leyendecker $37

Private Detective, 1944-1948 . . . . $4-8

Progressive Farmer Magazine, The
1946-1949 . . . . $6-8
1950's $4-6
1960's $2-5
    June 1952, Parrish $33

Puck
1877-1918 . . . . $16-32

Pure-bred Dogs
1889-1899 . . . . $15-22

Pure-bred Dogs (Continued)
1900-1939 . . . . $6-12
1940-1959 . . . . $4-8
1960- $2-5

Quick, 1949-1959 . . . . $5-10
    December 5, 1949, Autry $25
    February 20, 1950, Roy Rogers $32
    April 24, 1950, Cinderella Article $32
    May 19, 1952, Gen. MacArthur $25
    November 3, 1952, Eisenhower/Stevenson $25

Racing Pictorial, 1963-1964 . . . . $15-25

Radio and Television Mirror, Oct. 1941 . . . . $20

Radio Dial, 1930- $4-10

Radio Digest, *Feb. 1939, Vol. 1 #1.* $10

Radio Guide
1930's $22-32
1940's. $10-20
    March 30, 1935, Leah Raye $37
    January 11, 1936, Billie Trask $37

Radio Mirror 1930's $20-30

Radio News, 1930's $10

Radio Stars
1931-1934 . . . . $20-30

Radio & TV Mirror
1939-1956 . . . . $10-20
    Dec. 1939, Judy Garland $55

Radio Guide
    Oct. 13, 1934, D. Lamour $32
    Nov. 17, 1939, Gene Autry $20

Rail Age Magazine
1926. . . . . $15-20
1960-1967. . . . . $4-8

Railroad Stories, 1906- $3-10

Railway and Locomotive Historical Society, Inc. Bulletin
1921- $2-5

Rave, *December 1955, Clark Gable* $10

Readers Digest
1921-1929 . . . . $4-6
1930's $3-5
1940's $2-4
1950- $1-3

Real America, 1935 . . . . $4-8

Real Screen Fun
1934-1942 . . . . $3-8
  September 1934, Lupe Velez $22
  May 1941, Showgirl on cover $10

Redbook
1903-1909 . . . . $6-10
1910-1939 . . . . $4-6
1940-1959 . . . . $3-5
1960- $1-3
  December 1934, Carole Lombard $27

Red Cross Magazine
  June 1918, Rockwell $37
  Aug. 1917, WWII $15
  Oct. 1919 . . . . $15
  Oct. 1920 . . . . $15

Review of Reviews, The,
  1890-1899. . . . . $5-10
  1900-1936 . . . . $3-6

Rexall Magazine
1938-1939 . . . . $6-8
1940's $3-5
  October 1938, E. Bergen & C. McCarthy $15
  January 1944, Clark Gable $10

Rifle
Vol. #1-#100. . . . . $4
Vol. #101- $2-3

Ring Magazine
1926-1929 . . . . $22-27
1930's $16-22
1940 . . . . $10-15

Ringling Bros. & Barnum & Bailey Circus Magazine
1930's $22-32
1940's $15-20
1950's $10-15

Rogue, *Dec. 1960, Bob Hope, Bob Newhart* $15

Rolling Stone
1967 . . . . $100-200
1968 . . . . $75-100
1969-1971 . . . . $25-65
1972-1974 . . . . $10-20
1975-1979 . . . . $3-8
1980's $1-4
      #1, 1967, John Lennon/Grateful Dead $300
      #22, 1968, John Lennon $150
      #26, 1969, Jimi Hendrix/J. Joplin $100
      #38, 1969, Jim Morrison/J. Hendrix $120
      #39, 1969, Bryan Jones/B. Dylan $120
      #68, 1970, Hendrix Memmorial $100
      #69, 1970, Joplin Memorial $100
      #88, 1971, Morrison Memorial $100
      Sept. 22, 1977, Elvis $30

Romantic Movie Stories
1920's $42-62
1930's $27-42
      March 1934, Dorothy Jordan $60
      May 1935, Ginger Rogers $60
      November 1935, Ginger Rogers $47
      June 1936, Carole Lombard by Mozert $47

Rona Barrett's Hollywood
1970's $5-10

St. Nicholas
1873-1909 . . . . $10-20
1910-1941 . . . . $4-8

Saturday Evening Post

1877-1898 . . . . $17-22
1899-1939 . . . . $12-17
1940-1959 . . . . $7-11
1960- $3-7

    Aug. 6, 1912, Coles Phillips $20
    May 20, 1916, Rockwell's 1st Post Cover $50
    March 22, 1919, Courting Couple, Rockwell $42
    May 24, 1930, Gary Cooper $42
    Feb. 19, 1938, Rockwell. $17
    June 4, 1938, Rockwell. $22
    Oct. 8, 1938, Rockwell. $30
    Dec. 17, 1938, Rockwell $20
    March 18, 1939, Rockwell. $20
    July 8, 1939, Rockwell. $30
    Dec. 17, 1939, Rockwell. $30
    Nov. 29, 1941, Rockwell. $20
    Dec. 20, 1941, Rockwell. $20
    Feb. 7, 1942, Rockwell $20
    May 26, 1945, Rockwell $35
    Nov. 24, 1951, Rockwell. $20
    June 11, 1955, Rockwell. $22
    May 19, 1956, Rockwell , Eye Doctor $20
    Oct. 6, 1956, Rockwell/Adlai Stevenson $25
    Oct. 13, 1956, Rockwell/Eisenhower $20
    Dec. 29, 1956, Rockwell $30
    April 20, 1957, W. Spahr $20
    May 25, 1957, Rockwell $20
    June 29, 1957, Rockwell/Kirk Douglas $20
    June 28, 1958, Rockwell $25
    Nov. 8, 1958, Rockwell $20
    Oct. 24, 1959, Rockwell $20
    Feb. 13, 1960, Rockwell's own story $42
    July 30, 1966, Bob Dylan $15
    June 1, 1968, Bobby Kennedy $35

Scene, *Dec. 1959, Sophia Loren* $5

Science and Invention in Pictures

    June 1925 . . . . $27
    July 1925 . . . . $17
    August 1925 . . . . $27

Science and Mechanics
1930's $6-12
1940's $3-6
1950-1960 . . . . $1-3

Scientific American
1845-1899 . . . . $10-20
1900-1939 . . . . $6-12
1940-1959 . . . . $4-8
1960-. $1-4

Scoop, November 1942 . . . . $6

Screen Album
1935-1939 . . . . $16-27
1940's $11-16
1950's $6-11
    1935, Jean Harlow $75
    1938, Deanna Durbin $65
    1941, Deanna Durbin $50
    Winter 1947, June Allyson $38

Screen Book
1932-1939 . . . . $25-30
    April 1933, Katherine Hepburn $50
    March 1934, Ruby Keeler $55

Screen Facts
Issue #1-22 . . . . $10-20

Screen Guide
1930's $15-30
1940's $10-25
1950's $5-10
    October 1936, Ginger Rogers $42
    Nov. 1939, Clark Gable $37

Screenland
1923-1929 . . . . $30-40
1930-1939 . . . . $15-30
1940-1957 . . . . $10-20
1958-1970 . . . . $5-9
    Nov. 1929, Gretta Garbo $42
    Feb. 1934, Jean Harlow $55
    January 1943, Dorothy Lamour $33

Scribner's – December 1895

Scribner's
December 1897

Scribner's – April 1899

Scribner's – August 1899

Scribner's – October 1900

Scribner's – December 1900

Scribner's – December 1901

Scribner's
October 1904

Screen Life
1965-1967 . . . . $3-6
     November 1941, Gene Tierney $25
     September 1956, Debbie Reynolds $15

Screen Parade
     January 1958, Elvis $50
     June 1961, Elvis $35

Screen Play
     October 1931, Barbara Stanwyck, Jean Harlow $33
     July 1933, Mae West $17

Screen Romances
1931-1939 . . . . $15-20
1940's $10-15
1950's $5-10
     August 1931, Nancy Carroll $35
     Jan. 1932, Norma Shearer $40
     Nov. 1933, Harlow $32
     Sept. 1934, Ruby Keeler $35
     Oct. 1935 , Claudette Colbert $25
     Aug. 1936, Shirley Temple $40
     Oct. 1936 . . . . $35
     Dec. 1936, Dionne Quints $45
     Oct. 1937, Greta Garbo $32
     Nov. 1937, Shirley Temple $40
     May 1940, Zorina & Richard Greene $24
     July 1940, L. Olivier & Greer Garson $23
     June 1942, Lamour/Denning $32
     Aug. 1942, Darnell/Shepperd $35
     Jan. 1943, Blair/Ameche $32
     September 1944, Gary Cooper $25
     Oct. 1945, Shirley Temple $20

Screen Romances Album, *1930, Janet Gaynor* $50-75

Screen Songs, *Oct. 1948, Bob Hope* $5

Screen Stars
1944-1947 . . . . $8-15
     February 1945, Errol Flynn $32
     February 1946, Rita Hayworth $20
     May 1946, June Allyson $20
     January 1947, Janet Blair $20

Screen Stories

1948-1959 . . . . $5-10
1960-1971 . . . . $3-6
September 1948, Betty Grable $15
Jan. 1949 . . . . $25
March 1949, Cornel Wilde $25
February 1951, Liz Taylor $25
March 1951, V. Johnson,Wyman & Keel $15
June 1967, Monkees $22
August 1971, Lana Turner $10

Scribner's

1870-1899 . . . . $7-15
1900-1919 . . . . $5-10
1920-1930 . . . . $4-6
Dec. 1898, Parrish $65
Dec 1903, Parrish illustration $25
March 1905, Portraits of Indians $20
Feb. 1909, Indians of the Stone Houses $35
Jan. 1910, T. Roosevelt $20
Dec. 1911, Dicken's Children $20
Aug. 1912, Pierce Arrow Cover $33
Feb. 1913, Day of Motor Cover $20
July 1914, T. Roosevelt $15
Aug. 1914, The Rakish Brigantine $15

See

1942-1954 . . . . $5-10
July 1942, Jane Russell $37
July 1948, Barbara Nichols $15

Shadowplay, 1934 . . . . $15

Shadow, The

1931-1932 . . . . $70-77
1933-1939 . . . . $22-42
1940- $7-15

Shadowland
1920's $17-27

Shooting Times
1960-1961. . . . . $3
1961- $2
          June thru November, 1961. . . . . $5

Show Business Illustrated, 1961- $17-27
Only 10 Issues, All edited by Hugh Hefner

Sight & Sound, *April 1954, Garbo* $6

Silver Screen
1930's $27-37
1940's $22-32
1950's $10-20
1960-1972 . . . . $4-8
          April 1960, Elvis $32
Sir, *December 1952, Marilyn Monroe* $100

Sketch Christmas Number, The
          November 25, 1938 . . . . $35

Sky, 1936- $2-5

Sky Fighters
1933-1937. . . . . $27-37
1938-1943 . . . . $18-27

Smart Set
1900-1930 . . . . $8-15

Smiths Illustrated Pattern Bazaar, 1871- $10-20

Snowy Egret
1922-1939 . . . . $4-8
1940-1959 . . . . $2-5
1960- $1-3

Something To Do
1915. . . . . $6

Song Hits

Song Lyrics, January 1938 . . . . $15

Song Parade, *Aug. 1942, Glenn Miller* $10

Songs and Music, July 1941, Dorothy Lamour $8

Songs and Stars, Nov. 1957 . . . . $22

Soviet Russia Today

Spacemen, *Jan. 1963, Men from the Moon* $22

Spicy Detective Stories

Spicy Mystery Magazine

Spicy Stories, 1928- $10-20

Spinning Wheel, 1961- $3

Spider

Spinning Wheel
1945-1949 . . . . $3-5
1950's- $1-3

Sport
1940's $8-15
1950's $4-7
1960's $2-4
      June 1948, Joe Louis $25
      Aug. 1948, Musial $25
      Sept. 1948, Williams/Dimagio $25
      October 1948, Lou Gehrig $25
      August 1960, Mickey Mantle $22
      May 1967, Koufax & Clemente $15

Sports Afield
1887-1899 . . . . $10-15
1900-1929 . . . . $5-10
1930-1949 . . . . $3-6
1950-1959 . . . . $2-5
1960- $1-4

Sports Illustrated
1955-1957 . . . . $8-15
1958-1960 . . . . $5-10
1961- $1-5
      1949, Vol. 1 No. 1 . . . . $110
      Aug. 16, 1954, Night Baseball $210
      Aug. 23, 1954, Golf Bags $210
      April 11, 1955, Mays/Durocher $80
      April 18, 1955, Al Rosen $80
      June 27, 1955, Duke Snider $30
      July 11, 1955, Yogi Berra $30
      Aug. 1, 1955, Ted Williams $75
      May 14, 1956, Al Kaline $30
      June 18, 1956, Mantle $75
      Oct. 1, 1956, World Series $50
      Oct. 29, 1956, P. Hornung $30
      July 8, 1957, Musial $44
      Aug. 10, 1959, Fox/Apancio $30
      Oct. 2, 1961, R. Maris $44

Sports Illustrated (Continued)

July 2, 1962, Mantle $44
March 4, 1963, Koufax $20
June 10, 1963, Cassius Clay $25
1964, Swimsuit Issue $65
Oct. 10, 1966, F. Robinson/B. Robinson $20
July 3, 1967, Clemente $25
Aug. 21, 1967, Yaz Trewski $25
Jan. 22, 1968, Lombardi $25
Sept. 8, 1969, Rose/Ernie Banks $25
April 15, 1974, H. Aaron $25
Nov. 28, 1977, Larry Bird/Cheerleaders $30
Dec. 22, 1982, W.Gretzky, Sportsman of the Year ... $25
Jan. 3, 1983, W. Gretzky $25
May 2, 1983, Larry Bird in Playoffs $25
July 23, 1983, Michael Jordan Olympics $25
Nov. 28, 1983, Michael Jordan & Sam Perkins $44
Special Issue 1984, Kosar/Marino $35
Jan. 23, 1984, Wayne Gretzky $20
Aug. 27, 1984, Pete Rose $35

Sportsman, May 1956. .... $3

Sporty, Lew Burdette $7

Spot The Entertaining Picture Magazine, Nov. 1941 ..... $8

Stag, 1962-1966. .... $3

Stage & Screen, April 1936. .... $44

Stage, the Magazine for After Dark
April 1939, Bette Davis & Brian Aherne $10
June 1939, Raymond Massey $10

Student and Schoolmate, 1858- $5-15

Success
1898-1907 .... $3-10

Successful Farming
1902-1919 . . . . $5-10
1920-1939 . . . . $4-8
1930-1949 . . . . $3-5
1950- $2-4

Sunday Illus. Magazine of the Sunday Sentinel
1915-1916 . . . . $5-8
      Aug. 8, 1915, Coney Island by Cady $15
      Nov. 21, 1915, Gene Pressler $15

Sunset, *Sept. 1935, Dionne Quints* $10

SunShine, 1900 . . . . $16

Sunshine and Health Magazine
1945-1949 . . . . $5-6
1950-51 . . . . $2-4

Stylist, The, 1933 . . . . $10

Tab Magazine, *August 1942, 1st Issue* $25

Taboo, 1949-1950 . . . . $8-10

Tales of Vodoo, 1968, issue #32 . . . . $5

Teen Screen Magazine
      November 1961, Elvis $22

Television Life, Jan. 1954 . . . . $22

Terror Tales
1934-1938 . . . . $55-78
1939-1941 . . . . $35-55

Texas Rangers Magazine, 1950 . . . . $5-10

Theatre Arts
      Nov. 1950, Boris Karloff $65

Thimk
Vol. 1, No.'s 1-6 . . . . $27-55

This Was Hollywood
Issues #1 & #2 . . . . $22

This Week
1940's $4-6
1950's $3-5
1960's $2-4

3-D Movie Magazine
#1 Sept. 1953, Marilyn Monroe $130
#3, Jane Powell $160

3-D Screen, *#1 – 1953, Jane Russell* $110

Thrilling Mystery
Sept. 1936 . . . . $78
Sept. 1938 . . . . $70
March 1940 . . . . $60

Time
1930's $5-10
1940's $4-8
1950's $3-6
1960's $2-5
1970's $1-3
Dec. 27, 1937, Disney $42
Nov. 18, 1940, Disney's Fantasia $32
Oct. 4, 1948, DiMaggio $20
April 10, 1950, T. Williams $10
July 26, 1954, W. Mays $10
Aug. 8, 1955, Campy $10
May 20, 1974, Nixon $15

Tobacco World, 1902 . . . . $20

Today's Woman, 1954-1959 . . . . $5-10

Top Secret, *Feb. 1958, Kitt, Garbo, Brando, Dimaggio* $8

Town and Country
1941- $5-10

Town Journal, 1954-1956. .... $3

Trail and Timberline, 1918- $2-5

Trains, 1940- $3-10

Travel, *Dec. 1915, Santa Cover* $27

Travel Tykes Weekly, 1939 .... $10

True, *September 1976, Joe Namath* $15

True Comics, *May 1948, DiMaggio* $27

True Confessions 1935-. $4-6

True Detective, *Dec. 1933, Pretty Boy Floyd* $27

True Mystic Confessions, *1937 (1st issue)* $15

True Story
1936-1942 .... $5-10
1943- $2-6
　　　 Nov. 1951, M. Monroe $20

Truth, 1881- $17-32

TV & Radio Mirror, 1957-1969 .... $6-10

TV & Movie Screen
　　　 February 1960, Elvis $20
　　　 March 1959, Elvis $27
　　　 October 1958, Elvis $32

TV Dial
　　　 Vol. 2 No. 3, Jan. 19, 1952, Red Skelton $32
　　　 Vol. 2 No. 36, Sept. 20, 1952, Martin/Lewis $32
　　　 Vol. 2 No. 40, Oct. 18, 1952, Lucy $50
　　　 Vol. 2 No. 45, Nov. 1, 1952, Jack Benny $32

TV Digest
>Oct. 29, 1949, Lone Ranger $35
>April 7, 1951, The Big Top Show $32
>Jan. 3, 1953, Jackie Gleason $22

TV Forecast, Aug. 9, 1952, Groucho Marx $35

TV Guide Note: Any issue with a special personality or topic on the cover will raise the price to the collector interested in that subject. TV Guides from regional sources before 1953 will start at $25 and many will go for much more.

1953-1956 . . . . $10-20
1957-1960 . . . . $8-15
1961-1969 . . . . $6-12
1970-1979 . . . . $5-10
>Nov. 6-12, 1948, Bob Smith & Howdy Doody $110
>Aug. 6-12, 1949, Captain Video $420
>Dec. 10-16, 1949, Jackie Gleason $320
>April 15-21, 1950, Jackie Robinson $75
>May 6-12, 1950, Hopalong Cassidy $210
>July 8-14, 1950, Williams/DiMaggio $110
>Sept. 2-8, 1950, Howdy Doody $180
>Jan. 25-31, 1952, Lucille Ball & Desi Arnaz $210
>March 7, 1952, A. Godfrey $25
>May 17, 1952, Gene Autry $50
>Sept. 25, 1953, George Reeves $320
>April 3, 1953, Lucille Ball's Baby on cover $320
>April 10, 1953, Jack Webb $75
>Sept. 8, 1956, Elvis $110
>Nov. 22, 1958, Reagan $70
>May 7, 1960, Elvis $55
>June 11, 1966, Gilligan Article $25
>Nov. 2, 1968, Mod Squad $25

TV Headliner, Sept. 1955, D. Reynolds & E. Fisher $15

TV People Magazine, Vol. 4 No. 3, June 1956 . . . . $20

TV Picture Life
1955-1959 . . . . $11-22
1960-1964 . . . . $5-10

TV Picture Yearbook, *1954, Lucy/Desi* $27

TV Radio Mirror
    March 1960 , Elvis $22
    August 1975, Michael Landon. $15

TV Radio Talk, *Nov. 1975, Rick Nelson* $15

TV Star Parade
1950's. $5-10
1960's. $2-5
    Fall 1951, Martin/Lewis $22
    April 1957, Elvis $27
    September 1957, Elvis $27
    Dec. 1970, Elvis $15

TV Western
1958-1960 . . . . $44-55

TV Western Roundup, *1957-* $8-17

TV World, *1959-1967.* $5-8

US
1977-1979 . . . . $5-10
1980's $3-6

U.S. News and World Report
1933-1939. . . . . $4-8
1940's $2-5
1950- $1-3

Utah Historical Quarterly, *1928-* $1-4

Venus, *Nov. 1973, 1st Issue* $15

Vicks Magazine
1878-1899. . . . . $4-8
1900- $2-5

Vogue
1930's $6-10
1940's $4-8
1950's $3-6

Walt Disney Magazine
Vol. 1 No. 1, 1956. . . . . $60
Vol. 1 No. 2, Spring 1956. . . . . $32
Vol. 2 No. 4-6, April 1957 . . . . $22
Vol. 3 No. 2, 1958 . . . . $22

War Aces, *Issue #3, 1941.* $27

War Cry, 1884- $2-10

War Birds, Nov. 1933 . . . . $37

Ward's Natural Science Bulletin, 1881- $1-5

Weekly Film Review
1930's $22-44
June 30, 1931, John Wayne $65
Feb. 11, 1932, Babe Ruth / M. Detrich $55
June 23, 1932, Mickey $55

Weird Tales
1923-1924 . . . . $55-80
1925-1929 . . . . $27-55
1930-1939 . . . . $18-33
1940-1954 . . . . $10-20

Western Publisher, June 1907 . . . . $5

Western Roundup
1st Issue, 1952, Autry/Brown/Elliott/Allen $22

Western Stars

#1 – Oct. 1949, Roy Rogers $70
#2, Gene Autry $60
#4 – Jan. 1950, Gene Autry $55
#6 – Sept. 1950, Allan "Rocky" Lane $55

What To Eat

1900's $5-10

Who's Who in Hollywood

1950's $10-20
1960's $8-15

Who's Who in Television . . .

Editions #1-7 . . . . $15-25
#9-#24 . . . . $5-10

Who's Who in Western Stars, 1950's $10-20
#4 – 1954, Roy Rogers $44

Who's Who of the Screen

1930-1931 . . . . $27-55

Wildest Westerns, #2-6 . . . . $25-35

Will Carleton's Magazine, 1894- $3-10

Wings, 1940's $15-20

Wisconsin Agriculturist & Farmer, 1945-1946. . . . . $3

Wisdom, 1956, Jonas Salk $32

Woman's Day

1937-1949 . . . . $6-8
1950's $4-6
1960's $3-5

Woman's Farm Journal, 1892- $3-10

Woman's Home Companion
1873-1919 . . . . $8-18
1920-1939 . . . . $5-10
1940-1959 . . . . $3-8
1960- $1-3
       Sept. 1933, Charlie Chaplin $27

Woman's World, 1901- $2-8

Womens Wear Daily, 1910- $2-10

Wonder Stories, April 1935 . . . . $22

World Today, 1896- $3-10

World's Work, The,
1892-1899 . . . . $5-10
1900- $3-8
       February 1923 . . . . $10
       July 1924 . . . . $10

Wrestling Life Magazine, June 1955 . . . . $27

Yank, 1941- $8-18

Yankee
       Dec. 1935, Parrish $44
       Dec. 1968, Parrish $27
       May 1977, Parrish $18

Young Ladies Journal, Feb. 1911 . . . . $22

Youth's Companion
1827-1899 . . . . $8-15
1900-1929 . . . . $5-10
1930-1941 . . . . $2-6
       October 20, 1898 . . . . $25
       February 24, 1916, Rockwell $44
       April 26, 1917, Rockwell $44
       February 1, 1921, Rockwell $22